I0448543

June 2013

TAX REFUNDS

IRS Is Exploring Verification Improvements, but Needs to Better Manage Risks

GAO-13-515

Highlights

Highlights of GAO-13-515, a report to the Committee on Finance, U.S. Senate

TAX REFUNDS

IRS Is Exploring Verification Improvements, but Needs to Better Manage Risks

Why GAO Did This Study

For tax year 2011, IRS matched over 140 million individual income tax returns against the 1.6 billion information returns it received from third parties such as employers. Generally, this match does not occur until well after refunds are issued. In early 2011 the then IRS Commissioner outlined a vision for a "Real Time Tax" system—a strategy to improve verification by matching third party information to income tax returns before refunds are issued, and IRS began exploring options for Real Time Tax later that year. GAO was asked to review IRS's strategy for exploring Real Time Tax. This report (1) describes when IRS receives and matches individual tax and information returns and (2) assesses the extent to which IRS is following leading practices for managing an exploratory effort of this importance. GAO reviewed IRS documents and guidance, including the Internal Revenue Manual, information return forms, and drafts of Real Time Tax planning documents. GAO generated descriptive data on the timing and volume of 25 information returns using IRS's Compliance Data Warehouse database. GAO identified leading practices on planning new initiatives at IRS using past GAO reports, internal control standards, and IRS documents.

What GAO Recommends

GAO recommends IRS identify time frames for the exploratory effort's critical phases and activities and develop a risk management framework for Real Time Tax. IRS agreed with our recommendations.

View GAO-13-515. For more information, contact James R.White at (202) 512-9110 or whitej@gao.gov.

What GAO Found

The Internal Revenue Service (IRS) receives few information returns before issuing most tax refunds. In 2012, IRS issued 50 percent of tax year 2011 refunds to individuals by the end of February, but had only received 3 percent of information returns. Most information returns are not received by IRS until after mid-April, and IRS conducts the first match of tax and information returns in July, with subsequent matches in February and May of the following year. For tax year 2010, over a year passed on average before IRS notified taxpayers of matching discrepancies, and IRS recognizes that this long time lag burdens taxpayers.

Timing of Refunds Issued Compared to Information Returns Received, Tax Year 2011

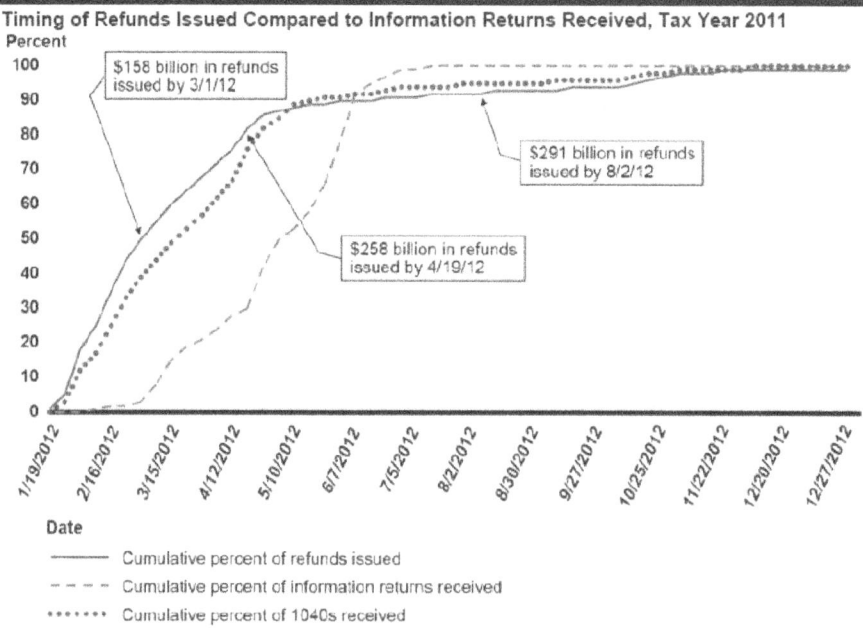

Source: GAO analysis of IRS data.

IRS is generally following leading practices in its Real Time Tax exploratory effort by, for example, dedicating a team and defining program goals. IRS did not develop an overall timeline because management views Real Time Tax as a broad goal, and officials wanted to avoid causing concern that IRS had already decided on a path. Without a timeline for the overall exploratory effort, IRS cannot know if its efforts will be completed in even the broad time frames IRS is considering, and Congress may not be able to determine what legislative action might be required. IRS officials stated that managing risk is a high priority, but they have not developed an overall risk management framework, as they are still in the early stages of the exploratory effort. They said they plan to further develop the strategy if IRS pursues Real Time Tax. Without systematically identifying and evaluating the risks of Real Time Tax options, IRS officials may miss critical factors that could complicate the effort. A record of prior risk analyses could help prevent unnecessarily repeating the same analyses.

_____ **United States Government Accountability Office**

Contents

Letter		1
	Background	3
	IRS Issued Most 2012 Refunds Months Before Receiving Information Returns and Matching Them to Tax Returns	8
	IRS Is Generally Following Leading Practices in Its Exploratory Efforts, but Has Not Developed a Timeline or Risk Management Framework	14
	Conclusions	22
	Recommendations for Executive Action	23
	Agency Comments	23
Appendix I	Objectives, Scope, and Methodology	25
Appendix II	Information Returns Used in Matching Against Individual Income Tax Returns	28
Appendix III	Leading Practices for Planning New Internal Revenue Service Initiatives	31
Appendix IV	Amendment Rates for Information Returns Used in Matching Against Individual Income Tax Returns	33
Appendix V	Comments from the Internal Revenue Service	34
Appendix VI	GAO Contact and Staff Acknowledgments	36

Tables

	Table 1: Key Questions for Real Time Tax and Examples of Early Options that IRS Is Considering[a]	15
	Table 2: Leading Practices for Planning New Internal Revenue Service Initiatives	31

Figures

Figure 1: Volume of Information Returns and as a Percentage of
Total Volume, Tax Year 2011   5

Figure 2: Key Dates for Information Returns, Filing Season 2012
(Tax Year 2011)   6

Figure 3: Timing of Refunds Issued Compared to Information
Returns Received, Tax Year 2011   9

Figure 4: Dates IRS Received 25 Information Returns and
Individual Income Tax Returns by Cumulative Percent of
Total Volume, Tax Year 2011   10

Figure 5: Timelines for Submission, Matching, and Taxpayer
Notification of Discrepancies for Information Returns and
Timely Filed Income Tax Returns, 2011 Filing Season
(Tax Year 2010)   13

Figure 6: Assessment of the Extent to Which IRS Is Implementing
Leading Practices in Its Real Time Tax Exploratory
Efforts   17

Figure 7: Real Time Tax Stakeholders   18

Figure 8: Amendment Rate for Information Returns, Tax Year 2011   33

Abbreviations

AUR	Automated Underreporter
CDW	Compliance Data Warehouse
IRS	Internal Revenue Service
RRB	Railroad Retirement Board
SSA	Social Security Administration

GAO U.S. GOVERNMENT ACCOUNTABILITY OFFICE

441 G St. N.W.
Washington, DC 20548

June 4, 2013

The Honorable Max Baucus
Chairman
The Honorable Orrin Hatch
Ranking Member
Committee on Finance
United States Senate

The Internal Revenue Service's (IRS) matching of tax returns to information provided to it by third parties is a powerful tool for helping ensure compliance with the tax laws. Doing so is a vast undertaking. For tax year 2011, IRS matched over 140 million individual income tax returns against the 1.6 billion third-party information returns, such as Form W-2, *Wage and Tax Statement*, it received from employers.[1] This matching helped IRS verify that taxpayers accurately reported their income and other information on their tax returns. While valuable, the matching process also has limitations. For example, information returns are not due to IRS until well after many taxpayers have filed their tax returns and received any refunds. As a consequence, IRS is unable to match tax returns to information returns before issuing most refunds. As a further consequence, when a mismatch shows a taxpayer underreported his or her tax liability, IRS cannot reduce the amount of any current refund. Instead, IRS must contact the taxpayer and try to collect the tax debt. This imposes additional burden on taxpayers and additional costs on IRS. Also, if the refund has been spent, taxpayers may not be able to readily pay the amount owed plus interest and any penalties.

In early 2011, the then IRS Commissioner outlined a vision for a "Real Time Tax" system—a strategy to improve verification by matching third-party information to income tax returns during the pre-refund screening process rather than after refunds are issued. In 2012, IRS launched a three-phase exploratory effort to assess the tradeoffs inherent in pursuing Real Time Tax. Moving the matching of third-party information during the pre-refund screening process could have significant impacts on taxpayers, third parties, and IRS processes and systems. It could also

---

[1]This volume of information returns excludes returns that were issued to business entities, such as corporations or partnerships.

require congressional action to authorize changes to the tax code, including, perhaps, changes to some information return due dates. Considerations associated with moving the due dates include whether third parties have the information they need before the current due dates and whether they would have sufficient time to detect and correct errors before reporting. IRS officials noted that they do not yet consider Real Time Tax a "project" and have not decided whether to pursue Real Time Tax.

Given the potential benefits and costs, you asked us to review IRS's strategy for exploring Real Time Tax. The objectives of this report are to (1) describe when IRS receives and matches individual tax and information returns and (2) assess the extent to which IRS is following leading practices for managing an exploratory effort of this importance at IRS.

To describe when IRS receives and matches individual tax and information returns, we reviewed IRS documents and guidance, including the *Internal Revenue Manual* and IRS information return forms.[2] We limited the scope of our review to the Form 1040 series[3] and the 25 information returns IRS officials said would likely be most relevant to matching to individual income tax returns under a Real Time Tax system.[4] These information returns are listed in appendix II. We generated descriptive statistics by accessing selected data elements from IRS's Compliance Data Warehouse (CDW) database, which provides a variety of tax return, enforcement, compliance, and other data. We assessed the reliability of CDW data by (1) performing electronic or manual testing of

---

[2]See appendix I for more information about our scope and methodology.

[3]The Form 1040 series includes, among others, Forms 1040 and 1040A, *U.S. Individual Income Tax Return*; 1040EZ, *Income Tax Return for Single And Joint Filers With No Dependents;* 1040-NR, *U.S. Nonresident Alien Income Tax Return*; 1040-PR, *Planilla para la Declaración de la Contribución Federal sobre el Trabajo por Cuenta Propia (Incluyendo el Crédito Tributario Adicional por Hijos para Residentes Bona Fide de Puerto Rico)*; and 1040-SS, *U.S. Self-Employment Tax Return (Including the Additional Child Tax Credit for Bona Fide Residents of Puerto Rico.)* The 1040-PR is the Spanish version of the 1040-SS. In addition, Form 1040-SS is for use by bona fide residents of the U.S. Virgin Islands, Guam, American Samoa, and the Commonwealth of the Northern Mariana Islands.

[4]We excluded certain information returns IRS officials said are not relevant to IRS's Real Time Tax exploratory effort, such as those issued to taxpayers with employer identification numbers, as well as Schedule K-1s. We also excluded other types of returns not used for matching against Form 1040s, such as Form FinCen 104, *Currency Transaction Report*.

required data elements to identify obvious errors, (2) reviewing existing information about the data and the system that produced them, and (3) interviewing agency officials knowledgeable about the data. We determined that the data were sufficiently reliable for the purposes of this report.

We reviewed our previous reports, *Standards for Internal Control in the Federal Government*,[5] and IRS documents, including the 2009 to 2013 *IRS Strategic Plan* to identify leading practices that we consider relevant for planning initiatives at IRS. The leading practices we identified do not represent the universe of practices that IRS could employ when planning a new initiative. We selected examples of leading practices that we judged to be important for IRS to consider during its Real Time Tax exploratory efforts. We discussed with IRS the practices on which we based our descriptions and assessments during the course of our audit work, and IRS agreed with our approach. To assess the extent to which IRS is following leading practices in its exploratory efforts, we reviewed IRS documents related to the Real Time Tax exploratory effort, all of which were predecisional and subject to change. Documents we reviewed included draft copies of the *Real Time Tax Conceptual Future Operating Model* and the *Real Time Tax Communications Strategy and Plan*. We then compared IRS efforts to the leading practices we identified. A description of the leading practices is detailed in appendix III.

We conducted this performance audit from August 2012 to June 2013 in accordance with generally accepted government auditing standards. Those standards require that we plan and perform the audit to obtain sufficient, appropriate evidence to provide a reasonable basis for our findings and conclusions based on our audit objectives. We believe that the evidence obtained provides a reasonable basis for our findings and conclusions based on our audit objectives.

Background

Third-party information reporting dramatically increases the accuracy of tax returns. Third parties—employers, banks, and others—report wages,

---

[5]GAO, *Standards for Internal Control in the Federal Government*, GAO/AIMD-00-21.3.1 (Washington, D.C.: Nov. 1, 1999).

interest, and other information to both taxpayers and IRS.[6] An IRS study of individual tax compliance found that in tax year 2006, taxpayers accurately reported over 90 percent of income with substantial information reporting requirements, such as interest and dividend income.[7] In contrast, the same study found taxpayers accurately reported only 44 percent of income subject to little or no information reporting, such as nonfarm sole proprietor income.

There are more than 40 different types of information returns, 25 of which are directly matched against income tax returns filed by individuals. According to IRS's analysis of tax year 2009 data,[8] most taxpayers receive at least one of three information return types: Form W-2, *Wage and Tax Statement*; Form 1099-G, *Certain Government Payments*; or Form 1098, *Mortgage Interest Statement*.[9] In terms of the volume of information returns IRS receives, a few types of returns accounted for the majority of returns in tax year 2011, as shown in figure 1.

---

[6]For purposes of this report, we use the term "provider" to refer to all third parties that provide information returns to IRS, including employers, corporations, partnerships, payroll providers, estates, trusts, financial institutions, educational institutions, and state and federal agencies.

[7]IRS, *Tax Gap for Tax Year 2006 Overview* (Washington, D.C.: Jan. 6, 2012). Accessed March 4, 2013, http://www.irs.gov/pub/newsroom/overview_tax_gap_2006.pdf.

[8]A tax year is the year in which the tax liability is incurred and the filing season year is the year in which the taxpayer files the tax return (usually the year after the tax year).

[9]Internal Revenue Service, *'Real Time' Tax System Opportunity: Briefing on Initial Baseline Analysis* (Washington, D.C.: Oct. 22, 2012).

Figure 1: Volume of Information Returns and as a Percentage of Total Volume, Tax Year 2011

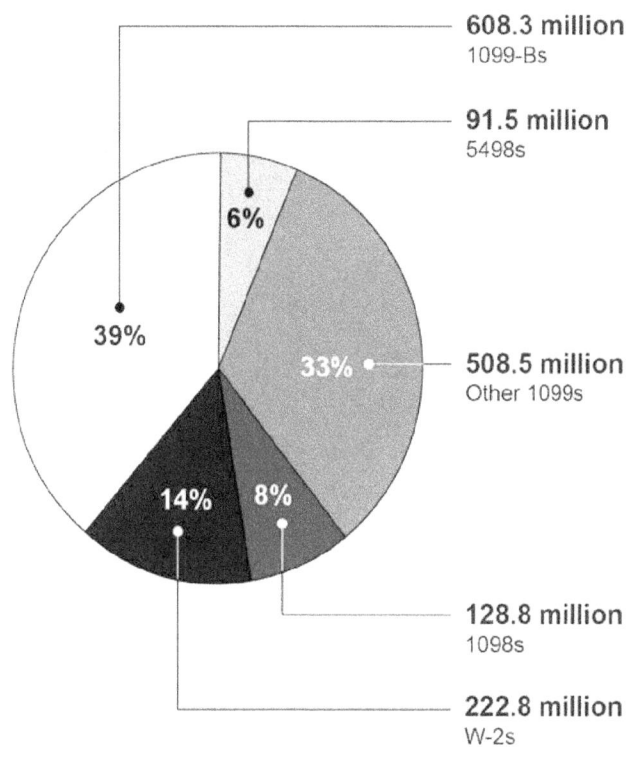

608.3 million
1099-Bs

91.5 million
5498s

508.5 million
Other 1099s

128.8 million
1098s

222.8 million
W-2s

Source: GAO analysis of IRS data.

Note: See appendix II for a list and descriptions of information returns. Analysis excludes information returns issued to taxpayers with employer identification numbers. Category 1099 includes 16 types of Form 1099, excluding the 1099-B, *Proceeds From Broker and Barter Exchange Transactions.* Category W-2 includes Form W-2, *Wage and Tax Statement,* and Form W-2G, *Certain Gambling Winnings.* Category 1098 includes Forms 1098, *Mortgage Interest Statement;* 1098-T, *Tuition Statement;* and 1098-E, *Student Loan Interest Statement.* Category 5498 includes Forms 5498, *IRA Contribution Information;* 5498-ESA, *Coverdell Education Savings Account Contribution Information;* and 5498-SA, *Health Savings Account, Archer Medical Savings Account or Medicare Advantage Medical Savings Account Information.*

Information returns are sent to taxpayers and IRS but the dates they are due to taxpayers differ from the dates they are due to IRS (see fig. 2). Furthermore, the dates most information returns are due to IRS are well after the start of the tax filing season.[10] Many taxpayers who expect refunds file early in the filing season to get their refunds as soon as possible. Due dates for information returns are established by statute and associated regulations. (For more information on information return due dates, see app. II.)

Figure 2: Key Dates for Information Returns, Filing Season 2012 (Tax Year 2011)

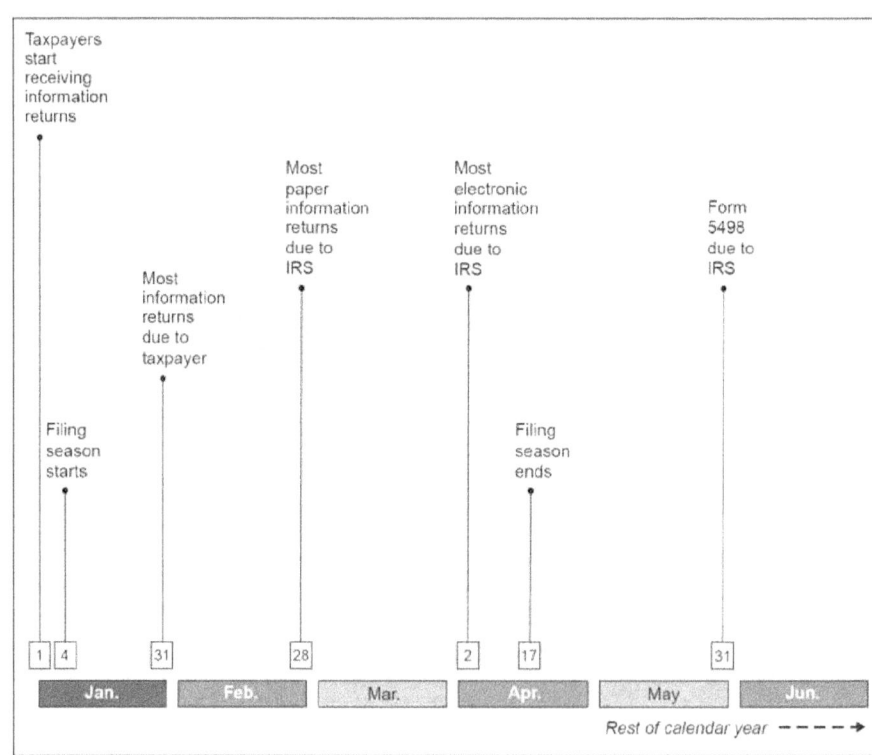

Source: GAO analysis of IRS documents.

Note: See appendix II for details on information return due dates.

About 97 percent of information returns for tax year 2011 issued to individuals that we analyzed were submitted to IRS electronically. For 22 of the 25 return types, the electronic submission rate was at least 99

---

[10]The filing season is when most taxpayers interact with IRS. Most taxpayers file their tax returns between January 1 and April 15, the deadline for filing individual income tax returns. If April 15 falls on a weekend or a holiday, the due date is the next business day.

percent. For 3 of the remaining return types, Forms W-2 had an electronic filing rate of 87 percent;[11] 1099-S, *Proceeds from Real Estate Transactions*, had a rate of 86 percent; and 1099-MISC, *Miscellaneous Income*, had a rate of 67 percent.

IRS uses what officials refer to as a "look-back" compliance model. Rather than holding refunds until all compliance checks can be completed, IRS issues refunds after doing some automated filtering of returns to detect fraud and correct obvious errors such as calculation mistakes and violations of eligibility limits for deductions and credits.[12] For 2013, IRS informed taxpayers that it would issue most refunds less than 21 days after receiving a tax return.

IRS's Automated Underreporter (AUR) program matches information returns to tax returns and pursues discrepancies. The AUR program conducts matches in three phases, following a staggered schedule in part to accommodate when it receives information returns and income tax returns. IRS conducts its first match in July for income tax returns filed by April 15; the second match in February of the following year for income tax returns received between April 16 and October 15; and the third match in May of the following year for income tax returns received after October 15. According to IRS, the first match is performed in July to allow for receipt of most information returns. IRS officials commented that matching dates are also affected by competing demands for the agency's information technology resources. When IRS identifies discrepancies it determines which cases to pursue and sends notices to taxpayers. These notices instruct the taxpayer to, at a minimum, contact IRS to resolve the discrepancy and in many instances will also propose the additional taxes

---

[11]Employers file Form W-2 with the Social Security Administration (SSA), which performs quality checks before submitting Form W-2 data to the IRS. The SSA sends all Form W-2 data electronically to IRS, although the original W-2 returns may be filed with SSA on paper or electronically. For tax year 2011, 87 percent of W-2 returns were filed electronically with SSA while 13 percent were filed on paper.

[12]IRS is granted math error authority in 26 U.S.C. § 6213(b). It can be used for certain purposes specified by Congress in 26 U.S.C. § 6213(g)(2) including correcting calculation errors and checking for other obvious noncompliance such as claims above income and credit limits. Without specific statutory authority, IRS cannot pursue assessment and collection activities without issuing a statutory notice of deficiency.

GAO-13-515 Real Time Tax

and penalties due from the taxpayer. Due to resource constraints, IRS does not pursue all discrepancies.[13]

At a high level, IRS's concept for Real Time Tax involves (1) matching electronically filed individual tax returns to third-party information returns; (2) notifying taxpayers of potential discrepancies; and (3) resolving discrepancies before issuing a refund. IRS officials noted that the agency would need to communicate quickly with taxpayers for the Real Time Tax concept to be feasible. However, officials noted quick communication is complicated by IRS efforts to protect taxpayers from so-called "phishing scams" and other email-related forms of fraud. As a precaution, IRS has only contacted taxpayers through regular mail and has instructed taxpayers not to respond to email messages purporting to be from IRS.

IRS Issued Most 2012 Refunds Months Before Receiving Information Returns and Matching Them to Tax Returns

Consistent with IRS's practice of issuing refunds promptly after a return is filed,[14] IRS issued 50 percent of 2012 refunds for tax year 2011 to individual taxpayers by the end of February, at which point only 3 percent of all information returns had been received.[15] By April 19, 2012, IRS had issued 82 percent of refunds to individual filers but had received only 30 percent of all information returns. By August 2, 2012, when IRS completed its first match of information return data to tax returns, IRS had issued 92 percent of refunds to individual taxpayers, as shown in figure 3.

---

[13]Not all discrepancies represent noncompliance (i.e., underpayment of taxes due). Some cases involve discrepancies that can be explained by taxpayers while others may be resolved without taxpayer contact. In addition, some discrepancy cases may be transferred to Examination for further review. IRS also identifies nonfilers by comparing information return data to individual income tax return data and routes these cases to either the Substitute for Return or Automated Substitute for Return programs. These programs were not within the scope of this review.

[14]If an individual files on time and is due a refund, the law requires IRS to refund any overpayment made by the individual within 45 days of the last day prescribed for filing the return. If IRS takes longer, IRS is required to pay interest beginning on the 46th day after the statutory due date for filing the return. 26 U.S.C. § 6611(e).

[15]For purposes of our analysis we use the term "received" to refer to the posting date when IRS posts tax return data to the master file, which represents when the tax return data are available for matching. Officials noted that IRS must cleanse the data prior to posting to IRS systems. This may include identifying and correcting incomplete or inaccurate data before posting the data to IRS systems.

Figure 3: Timing of Refunds Issued Compared to Information Returns Received, Tax Year 2011

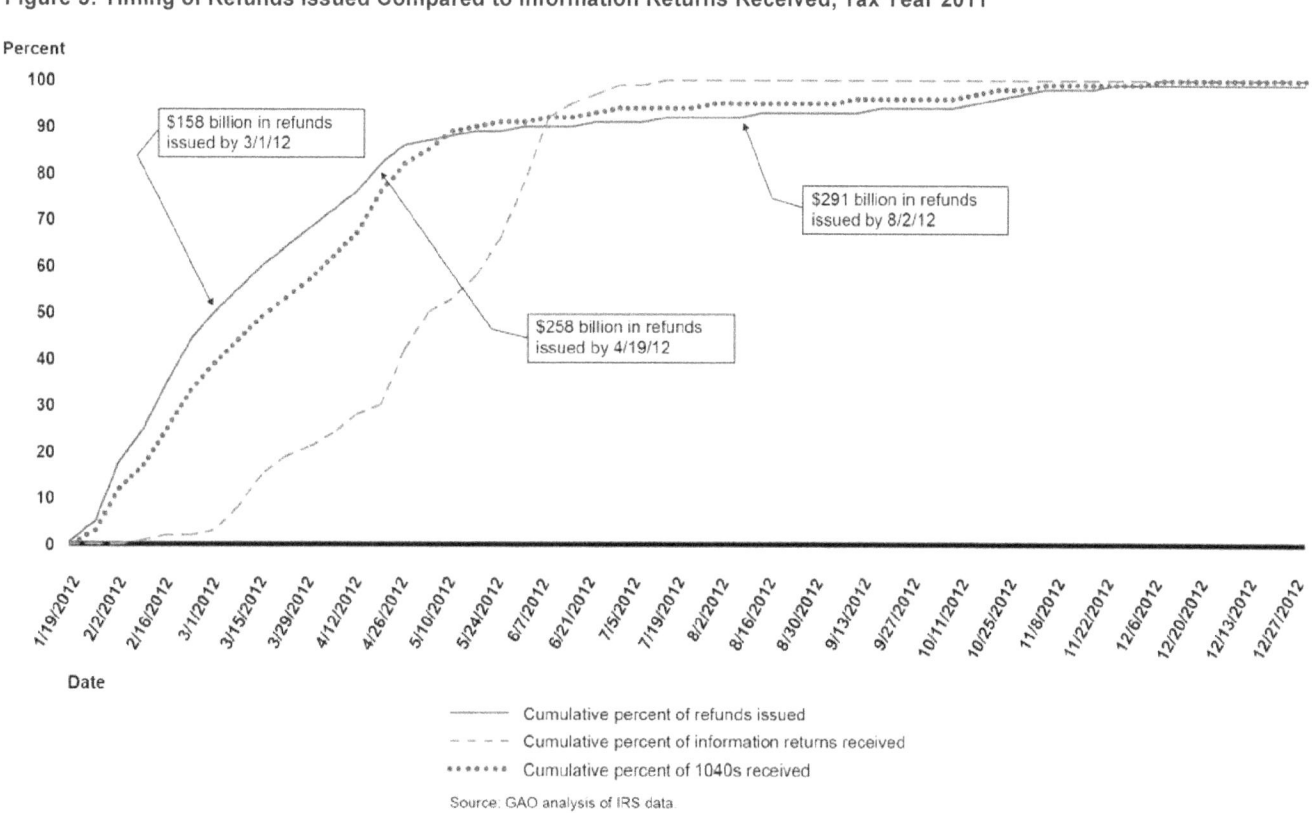

Percent

$158 billion in refunds issued by 3/1/12

$291 billion in refunds issued by 8/2/12

$258 billion in refunds issued by 4/19/12

Date

——— Cumulative percent of refunds issued

– – – – Cumulative percent of information returns received

•••••• Cumulative percent of 1040s received

Source: GAO analysis of IRS data.

Note: Dates shown above are for calendar year 2012, which corresponds to the filing season for tax year 2011 returns. Data reflect dates by which IRS posted tax return information to the master file, at which point data are available for matching. Officials noted that IRS must cleanse the data prior to posting to IRS systems. This may include identifying and correcting incomplete or inaccurate data before posting the data to IRS systems. See appendix I for details.

No Information Return Types Were Received in Significant Numbers Before the End of February

Figure 4 expands upon figure 3 to show that IRS did not receive any type of information return in significant numbers until March 2012. Of the 25 types of information returns represented in figure 4, IRS had received more than 30 percent of the submissions by March 1, 2012, for one form, Form 1099-G. For all other types, IRS had received less than 15 percent of submissions by March 1, 2012.

Figure 4: Dates IRS Received 25 Information Returns and Individual Income Tax Returns by Cumulative Percent of Total Volume, Tax Year 2011

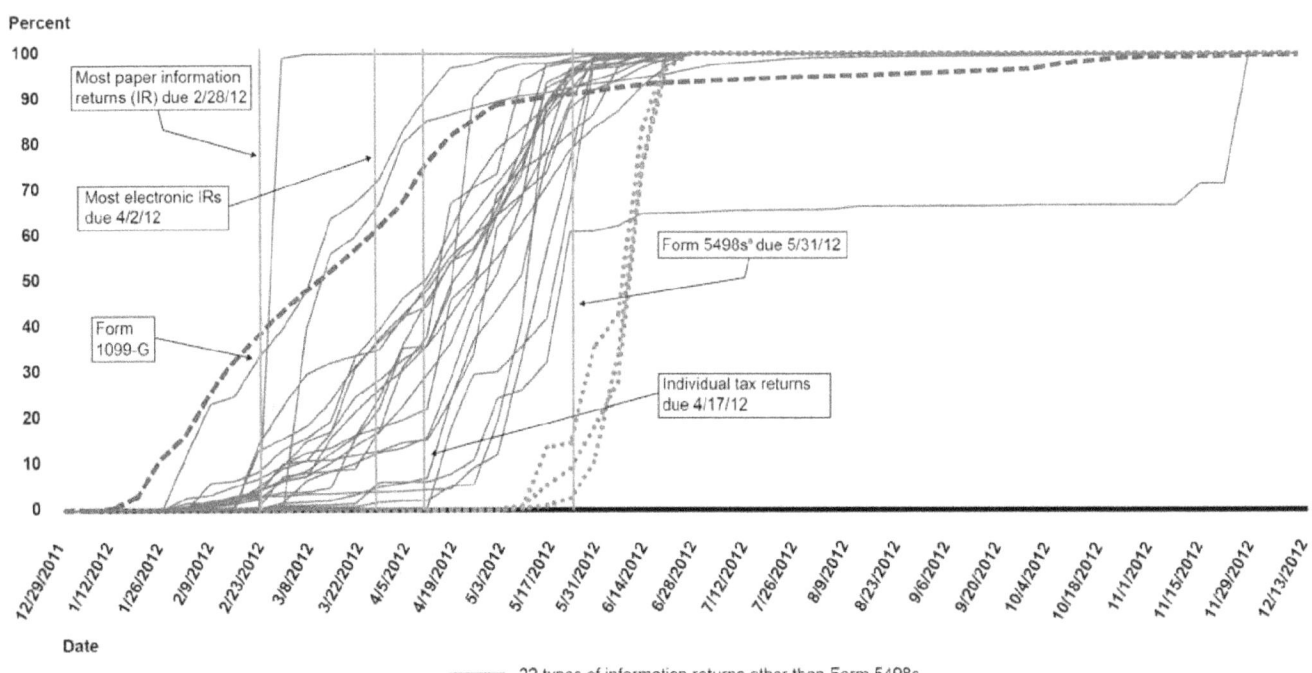

```
——— 22 types of information returns other than Form 5498s
▪ ▪ ▪ ▪ Individual tax returns
• • • • • 3 types of Form 5498s
```

Source: GAO analysis of IRS data.

Notes: The data include amended returns and returns designated as "unknown" at the time of our analysis. Amended and "unknown" returns accounted for 2 percent (33 million) of the total 1.6 billion information returns associated with individual tax filers that IRS received. Forms 5498 (the lines furthest to the right in the figure above) are due to IRS by May 31.

Dates shown above are for calendar year 2012, which corresponds to the filing season for tax year 2011 returns. Data reflect dates by which IRS posted tax return information to the master file, at which point data are available for matching. Officials noted that IRS must cleanse the data prior to posting to IRS systems. This may include identifying and correcting incomplete or inaccurate data before posting the data to IRS systems. See appendix I for details.

[a]Form 5498s include Forms 5498, *IRA Contribution Information*; 5498-ESA, *Coverdell Education Savings Account Contribution Information*; and 5498-SA, *Health Savings Account, Archer Medical Savings Account or Medicare Advantage Medical Savings Account Information*.

As shown in figure 4, IRS receives many information returns after their original due dates. To begin matching earlier in the year, one option is to move up information return due dates. However, without an understanding of why information returns are filed after they are due, simply moving the dates may not be effective. As discussed below, IRS frequently grants extensions to information return providers.

Filing Extensions Influence When IRS Receives Information Returns

Data from IRS did not indicate what proportion of the information returns arriving after due dates was attributable to filing extensions, but an official told us that the agency approved 371,000 requests for filing extensions from information return providers for tax year 2011.[16] According to IRS, information providers request extensions for reasons that include complex IRS regulations, changes in tax laws, and changes in information return forms. In focus groups held by IRS, some providers of more complex return types noted they automatically request a filing extension to allow time for taxpayers to review their copy of the information return and notify the provider of any needed corrections. Some providers said that they are hesitant to provide returns to IRS before hearing from taxpayers because IRS can levy penalties on providers that file forms with incorrect information.[17]

Amendment Rates Influence When Accurate Data Are Available for Matching

Moving information return due dates could affect the volume of information return amendments. Amendments are changed information returns resubmitted to IRS and the amendment rate is the percent of total information return volume attributed to amended, duplicate, or corrected returns received by IRS. In focus groups held by IRS, some information return providers noted that accelerating submission due dates for complex information returns would create challenges, as they often need to correct information in consultation with information return recipients before submitting data to IRS. We did not assess the volume or timing of corrections made by providers before sending information returns to IRS.

On average, information returns had an amendment rate of less than 0.4 percent. Only 3 of the 25 information returns we reviewed had amendment rates greater than 2 percent. While amendment rates for most information returns were low for tax year 2011, they still represented

---

[16]According to IRS, extensions submitted cover the payer and all the information return types they submit.

[17]Information providers face penalties if they fail to file correct information returns on or before the required filing date, they fail to include all the information required on the return, or they include incorrect information. 27 U.S.C. § 6721.

millions of returns. For example, the amendment rate for Form W-2 was only 0.94 percent, but this represented over 2 million of the 213 million W-2s for tax year 2011 that IRS received. One reason for low amendment rates may be providers' fear of penalties, as discussed above. Appendix IV provides additional information on amendment rates.

On Average, More Than a Year Passes Before IRS Notifies Taxpayers of Matching Discrepancies

For 2010 income tax returns which were filed starting in 2011, IRS took over 1 year (388 days), on average, to notify taxpayers about AUR discrepancies.[18] This is the elapsed time between when the taxpayer filed his or her income tax return and when IRS issued the first notice. The longest elapsed time was 763 days, just over 2 years. As a consequence, taxpayers may not be notified about a potential error until after filing the following year's return. IRS officials acknowledge that such a delay may be a burden to taxpayers and said they are interested in pursuing Real Time Tax in order to improve the taxpayer experience. The officials noted that the longer the time between filing an income tax return and receiving a notice, the harder it is for some people to locate the records or other information needed to understand the discrepancy, as well as to respond to IRS and resolve the issue.[19] In addition, if taxpayers spent their refund or tax savings they may not have funds set aside for an unexpected tax debt. Finally, penalties and interest may have accumulated, which increases the amount due. One of the goals of Real Time Tax would be to reduce the number of taxpayers facing these burdens by detecting and resolving discrepancies before refunds are issued.

IRS identified nearly 24 million 2010 income tax returns with discrepancies. According to IRS data, IRS selected about 22 percent (or 5.3 million) of these discrepant returns for review. After the review, IRS sent at least one notice to over 4 million of these taxpayers informing them of the discrepancy.

---

[18]The median elapsed time was 378 days. We analyzed discrepancy data including the timing of IRS's follow-up based on tax year 2010, the most recent year for which IRS had completed its matching process as of the date of our analysis, April 17, 2013. As of this date IRS had not yet conducted the third match for tax year 2011 returns.

[19]Taxpayers are required to keep such records under 26 U.S.C. § 6001 and its associated regulations under 26 C.F.R. 1.6001-1. For more specific information about recordkeeping for individuals, see IRS Pub. 552, *Recordkeeping for Individuals* (Rev. January 2011). Under 26 U.S.C. § 6501, the IRS can assess additional tax within 3 years after a return was filed. This has given rise to the general principle that taxpayers should maintain their tax records for at least 3 years in most circumstances.

Figure 5 shows timelines for 2011 return processing, matching, and taxpayer notification based on the first match at the end of July. The left side of the graphic illustrates when IRS and taxpayers receive most information returns, and the right side illustrates when IRS begins notifying taxpayers of discrepancies.

Figure 5: Timelines for Submission, Matching, and Taxpayer Notification of Discrepancies for Information Returns and Timely Filed Income Tax Returns, 2011 Filing Season (Tax Year 2010)

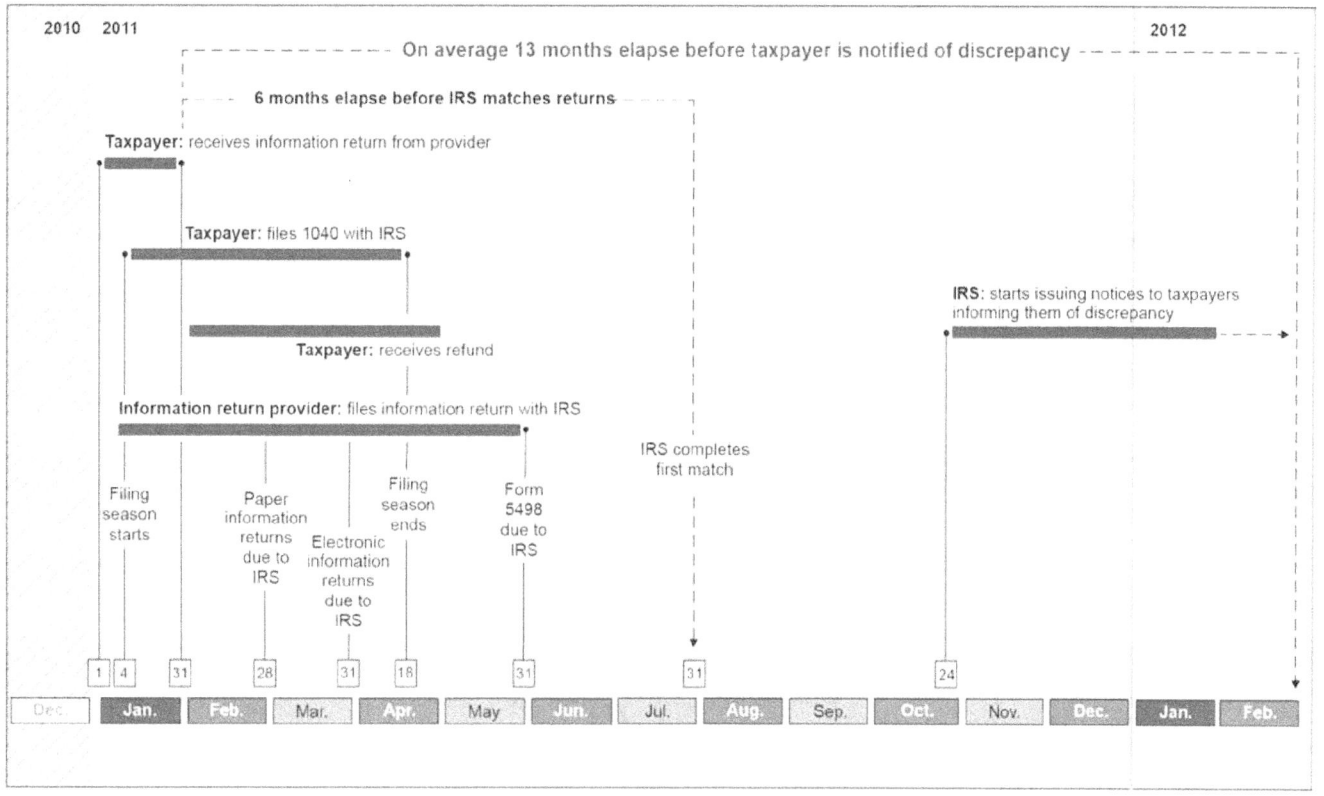

Source: GAO analysis of IRS documents

Note: This timeline assumes taxpayers started filing their income tax returns at the beginning of January, and IRS includes these returns in the first match conducted in July. Some activity occurs outside of the time frames depicted here. See appendix II for details on information return due dates.

IRS Is Generally Following Leading Practices in Its Exploratory Efforts, but Has Not Developed a Timeline or Risk Management Framework

IRS Is Exploring Options Before Deciding Whether to Pursue Real Time Tax

IRS officials and the planning documents they have developed make it clear that Real Time Tax is an exploratory effort. IRS officials emphasized that they have made no final decisions regarding Real Time Tax and that they do not perceive it as a "project" at this time. As part of the exploratory effort, IRS is collecting data to understand the potential disruptions to taxpayers and information return providers that could result should IRS implement a Real Time Tax system. Officials are also seeking to understand whether doing so would be an improvement over current processes, particularly AUR and accelerated matching for wage and withholding data. IRS is conducting tests to determine potential benefits, including whether IRS could match information returns at the time taxpayers file their tax returns in a Real Time Tax environment.

IRS officials are analyzing six key questions they see at the heart of the Real Time Tax concept. For each question, IRS has begun developing a list of options and is assessing them (see table 1). Officials stressed that they have made no final decisions regarding which options, if any, they may pursue.

Table 1: Key Questions for Real Time Tax and Examples of Early Options that IRS Is Considering[a]

Key question	Early option examples
Data. What can IRS do to improve the timeliness, accuracy, and availability of information returns?	Moving information return deadlines closer to January 31[b] or requiring providers to send information returns to taxpayers and IRS at the same time.
Matching. How will IRS perform matching and decide when resolution is required?	Using other data sources (e.g., state quarterly unemployment wage information) when a direct match is not successful, or using risk-based analytical rules for returns without data corroboration, such as past filing or compliance history and fraud patterns.
Identity. How will IRS validate the identity of taxpayers?	Matching identity information at the time of filing using taxpayer information, information returns, and/or other authentication solutions. If identity validation is insufficient, IRS would reject electronically filed (e-filed) returns or apply alternative identity theft treatments.
Notification. How will IRS notify the correct party to support issue resolution in the event of a discrepancy?	If data support identity validation, IRS is considering how to notify the taxpayer with information on discrepancies through notifications via tax software, email/secure notification, or paper for paper filers.
Resolution. How will the taxpayer resolve a discrepancy and what tools will be provided?	Providing self-service tools and customer service to help taxpayers investigate and resolve discrepancies, and having the taxpayer refile the return with revised information. If the discrepancy cannot be resolved or the taxpayer believes the original submission is accurate, IRS is exploring ways in which taxpayers can direct IRS to process the original return.
Return Preparers. How will return preparers assist their clients in resolving mismatch notifications?	Revising language on the Form 1040 to authorize tax preparers to view mismatch notifications from IRS.

Source: IRS draft *Conceptual Future Operating Model.*

Note: This table is not exhaustive of the options IRS is considering, and IRS officials noted they have not made final decisions regarding which options to pursue. We have not assessed the potential costs and benefits of any of the early options.

[a]Key questions and early options are listed in IRS's draft *Conceptual Future Operating Model*. This October 4, 2012, draft is predecisional, and IRS will update it as IRS completes additional analysis.

[b]According to IRS, it does not currently have legislative authority to move some deadlines for information returns.

Each option presents challenges to IRS as it considers how a Real Time Tax system might operate. For example, as noted previously, moving information return due dates to earlier in the filing season may affect amendment rates for some types of information returns.

IRS is exploring options using a three-phased approach that began in 2011. IRS focused its Phase 1 efforts on envisioning the taxpayer experience, incorporating input from internal and external stakeholders. During this phase, IRS held focus group meetings with stakeholders and developed a conceptual model for Real Time Tax. Phase 2 is exploring options for how business processes might change, and includes a gap analysis which considers how business operations work now versus how they may work if Real Time Tax was implemented. IRS officials told us they anticipate completing Phase 2 by the end of April 2013. If IRS proceeds to Phase 3, it will focus on determining what operational and information technology infrastructure changes will be needed. As documented in the draft *Conceptual Future Operating Model*, Phase 3 would include

- developing a roadmap for the proof of concept and implementation;

- comparing Real Time Tax work streams with IRS's long-term enterprise roadmap; and

- evaluating competing demands for resources and facilitating decision making around key investments supporting Real Time Tax.

Exploratory Efforts Generally Follow Leading Practices, but Plans Lack a Documented Timeline and Risk Management Framework

Figure 6 shows that IRS is following four of the six leading practices we used as criteria for assessing IRS's exploratory efforts, and plans to implement the other two practices. Appendix III explains the practices in more detail and the sources we used to develop the leading practices. These criteria are drawn from our previous reports, IRS policy guidance, and other sources.

Figure 6: Assessment of the Extent to Which IRS Is Implementing Leading Practices in Its Real Time Tax Exploratory Efforts

Leading Practices	Status	
Dedicate a team	Implementing	➡
Define program goals	Implementing	➡
Plan for performance measurement	Implementing	➡
Establish a timeline for the planning effort	Planning to implement- Actions needed	⇨ ★
Establish a risk management framework	Planning to implement- Actions needed	⇨ ★
Establish an internal and external communications strategy	Implementing	➡

➡ Implementing. IRS officials provided evidence that they are implementing the leading practice.

★ Actions needed. GAO recommends additional or continued action in the area.

⇨ Planning to implement. IRS officials provided evidence that they plan to implement the leading practice.

Source: GAO analysis of IRS documents and agency official interviews.

IRS Dedicated a Team

The Commissioner's Office created a team to lead IRS's Real Time Tax exploratory efforts. The team is comprised of Real Time Tax executives from the Wage and Investment Division and Information Technology organization; a core team of senior staff who work under the direction of the Real Time Tax executives to lead the exploratory effort; a support network of subject matter experts throughout IRS; and contractors. While some core team members and subject matter experts have transitioned on and off the effort to meet other organizational needs, IRS officials and core team members said that they have developed strategies to ensure the effort's leadership is consistent and that it has the necessary knowledge and skills. Core team members and other IRS officials confirmed that IRS provides overlapping assignments to allow for team members transitioning off the core team to brief incoming members on the history and progress of the effort. As discussed in more detail below, the core team has also identified external and internal stakeholders (see fig. 7).

Figure 7: Real Time Tax Stakeholders

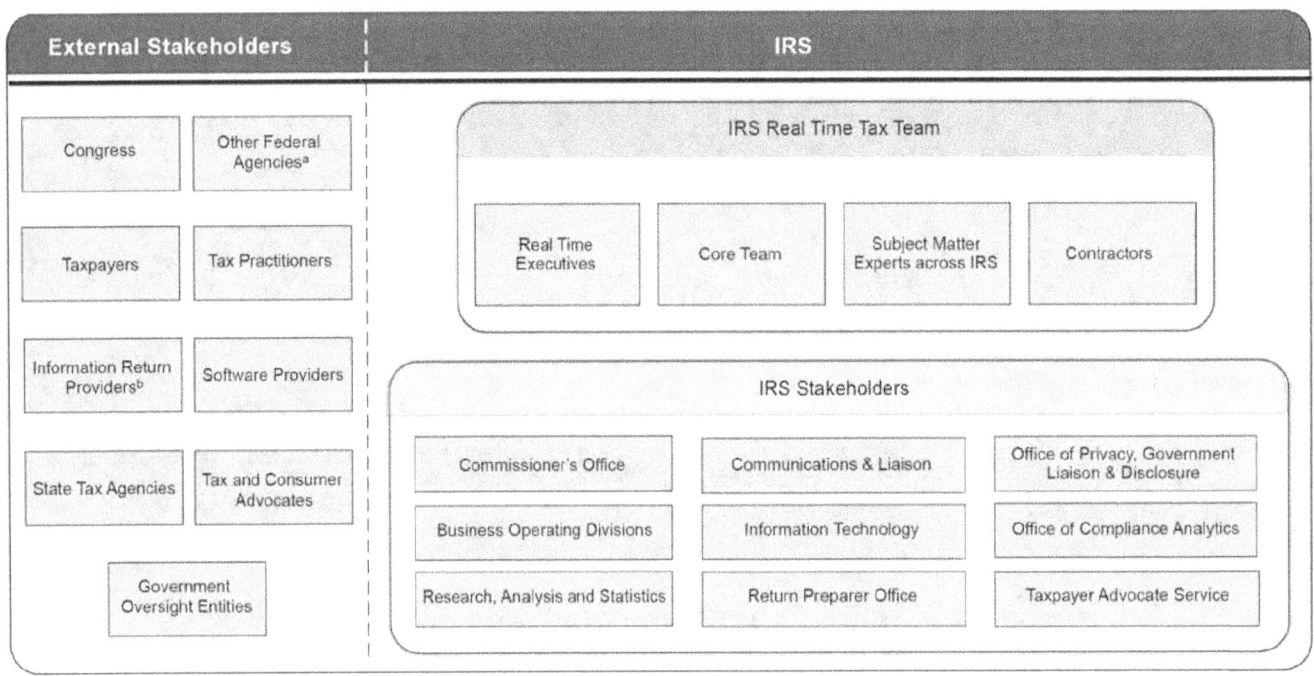

Source: GAO analysis of IRS documents.

[a]Federal agencies include the Office of Management and Budget and other agencies.

[b]Information return providers refer to all third parties that provide information returns to IRS, including employers, corporations, partnerships, payroll providers, estates, trusts, financial institutions, educational institutions, and state and federal agencies.

IRS Defined Program Goals

Key IRS stakeholders identified a vision and program goals for Real Time Tax that link to IRS's mission and consider taxpayer burden. For example, the draft *Conceptual Future Operating Model* documents IRS's vision to reduce taxpayer burden, improve compliance, and increase efficiency. IRS documents specify the following guiding principles and overall program goals for Real Time Tax:

- Minimize taxpayer burden by including measures to simplify the tax filing experience and not introducing changes that increase the burden for the majority of taxpayers.

- Build for the future by developing Real Time Tax with a long-term focus and implementing it with a phased approach that provides incremental benefits in the near-term.

- Leverage tax industry partners to help drive a successful Real Time Tax model.

- Mitigate vulnerabilities to identity theft and fraud to reduce the risk of IRS issuing credits and refunds to identity thieves and other fraudsters.

IRS has particularly emphasized the importance of minimizing taxpayer burden. In addition to identifying it as a guiding principle, officials said that, if they proceed, they will use statistical modeling to better understand the Real Time Tax system's potential effects on taxpayers.

The guiding principles outlined in the draft *Conceptual Future Operating Model* link closely with IRS's mission to provide taxpayers top-quality service while enforcing the law and meeting the agency's performance goals and objectives. Officials told us the core team has provided input for IRS's next strategic plan.

IRS Began Planning for Performance Measurement

IRS officials have begun planning for performance measurement and have taken steps such as conducting a baseline analysis, hypothesis testing, and considering performance measures. For example, IRS conducted a baseline analysis to understand the current volume, timing, filing patterns, and concentrations of tax filing activity for tax year 2009. During Phase 2, officials said that the core team is using statistical modeling to test possible Real Time Tax models to better understand their potential effects. These tests will help them understand whether they can match information return data at the time individuals file their tax returns and the extent to which IRS can notify taxpayers of a discrepancy at the time of filing. Officials noted that they are still determining what data will be needed to assess Real Time Tax, and whether such a system can provide benefits greater than those IRS and taxpayers receive under the current system. Officials consider it too early in the exploratory effort to define performance outcomes, but anticipate doing this as Real Time Tax exploration and planning progress.

IRS Documented Time Frames for Communicating with Stakeholders and Testing Matching Capabilities, but Has Not Developed a Timeline for the Overall Exploratory Effort

IRS documented time frames for its communication strategy and for evaluating matching capabilities, but has not developed a timeline for the exploratory efforts' critical phases and essential activities. The draft *Communications Strategy and Plan* documents a high-level timeline for implementing IRS's stakeholder communications strategy. IRS also documented time frames for live tests that began in March 2013 that will help officials understand whether IRS can match information return data to simple tax returns at the time of filing. However, while officials noted that the core team has a general idea about how long each planning phase should take, IRS has not developed a timeline or planned interim milestones for its overall exploratory effort. Officials noted that IRS management views Real Time Tax as a broad goal, and the core team did not set milestone dates to avoid causing concern among the stakeholder community that IRS has already decided on a path for Real Time Tax. Also, officials said that they want to conduct additional tests before planning next steps and then use the results of those tests to help determine if IRS should proceed with Phase 3.

As we have stated in prior reports, the demand for transparency and accountability is a fact that needs to be accepted in an exploratory effort of this magnitude.[20] Establishing a timeline that includes critical phases and essential activities that need to be completed by particular dates to achieve results is important for accountability and success in implementing a new exploratory effort. A full range of stakeholders and interested parties, including Congress, are concerned not only with what results are to be achieved, but also which processes are to be used to achieve those results. Also, an exploratory effort can build momentum internally and externally by demonstrating progress towards these goals.

We recognize that IRS's planned time frames and milestones may evolve as it learns from its exploratory efforts. Also, it may not be feasible for IRS to develop a detailed timeline for the Real Time Tax initiative, as planning efforts are still ongoing and officials have not decided whether to pursue Real Time Tax or how to structure it. At this early stage, it may make sense for IRS to identify contingency-based time frames rather than firm dates for the exploratory effort. However, having a documented timeline

---

[20]GAO, *Foreign Account Reporting Requirements: IRS Needs to Further Develop Risk, Compliance, and Cost Plans,* GAO-12-484 (Washington, D.C.: Apr. 16, 2012) and *Results-Oriented Cultures: Implementation Steps to Assist Mergers and Organizational Transformations,* GAO-03-669 (Washington, D.C.: July 2, 2003).

that identifies critical phases and milestones for essential activities—such as time frames for developing the "proof of concept" in Phase 3—could help IRS and Congress assess the progress of the exploratory efforts. Without a timeline for the overall exploratory effort, planning may go on endlessly, and IRS cannot know if its efforts are on track or will be completed in even the broad time frames IRS is considering. In addition, Congress may not be able to determine what legislative action may be needed.

IRS Has Not Yet Developed a Risk Management Framework

IRS officials stated that managing risk is a high priority for IRS, but while they have documented potential risks to Phase 2 testing, they have not developed an overall risk management framework for Real Time Tax. A risk management framework helps ensure that managers systematically identify, analyze, and manage risks. A documented risk management framework articulates what managers have done to analyze the consequences of identified risks and the likelihood they will occur, as well as to assess alternatives to mitigate risk.[21] Leading practices suggest that a risk management framework should be developed early so that relevant risks are identified and managed, and that the framework should evolve and be reviewed on an ongoing basis. Such a framework could help IRS identify and mitigate the risks stemming from options it is considering for Real Time Tax, including the risks of moving information return due dates and communicating electronically with taxpayers.

Officials stated they have not yet developed a risk management framework because they are still in the early stages of their exploratory efforts. Nevertheless, an IRS official stated that officials discuss potential risks for Real Time Tax regularly and that they are developing descriptions of "pros and cons" of the different approaches. IRS officials plan to further develop the risk strategy if IRS decides to pursue Real Time Tax.

Without systematically identifying and evaluating the risks of Real Time Tax options, IRS officials may miss critical factors that could complicate the effort, including the potential costs to IRS, taxpayers, and other stakeholders. Furthermore, without a documented record of risk discussions, IRS may lose its knowledge of what risks and mitigations

---

[21]Cost-benefit analysis is also critical in assessing alternatives, because it links the benefits derived from risk-reducing alternatives to the costs associated with implementing and maintaining them.

have been analyzed. For an effort that cuts across as many IRS functions as Real Time Tax and will likely take years to implement, a record of prior risk analyses could help prevent unnecessarily repeating the same analyses.

IRS Developed a Communication Strategy

IRS developed a communication strategy that identifies internal and external stakeholders, defines stakeholder communication needs, identifies communication media, and describes how IRS plans to communicate its Real Time Tax efforts to stakeholders. In its draft *Communications Strategy and Plan*, IRS developed talking points to describe its vision for Real Time Tax and to explain what a possible Real Time Tax system does not include. For example, IRS officials have stated that Real Time Tax will not involve a prefill option (where IRS prepopulates tax returns) or replace all compliance activity that occurs after the filing season, such as AUR. The draft *Communications Strategy and Plan* also states that IRS will work collaboratively with external stakeholders to outline the vision for Real Time Tax. To obtain the views of external stakeholders on potential frameworks for Real Time Tax, IRS held two public meetings and six focus groups involving individuals representing consumer groups, tax return preparers, the software industry, oversight agencies, payroll providers, and state revenue departments. IRS plans to continue activities aimed at increasing the public's awareness and understanding of the Real Time Tax exploratory effort. These activities may include responding to media inquiries, posting information to the IRS website, and sending IRS officials to speaking engagements.

Conclusions

Real Time Tax has the potential to provide substantial benefits, including reducing taxpayer burden and improving compliance by moving some information matching earlier in the tax season. However, it also may require significant and possibly costly changes to tax administration and impose new burdens on third parties. Careful consideration of risks and alternatives for mitigating those risks is crucial in weighing the potential benefits and costs of Real Time Tax options. While IRS has taken important steps in exploring the feasibility of Real Time Tax, much remains unknown because the exploratory effort is still underway. IRS has not yet developed time frames for the exploratory effort's critical phases and essential activities, and we anticipate IRS may revise time frames as it obtains new information from its exploratory efforts. In addition, IRS has not created a risk management framework, which would provide valuable information about potential costs and benefits to IRS management. Given the potential scope of a Real Time Tax system, both agreed-upon time frames and a record of risk management considerations are likely to be important management tools that will help inform IRS management's decisions about the future of Real Time Tax and help Congress oversee IRS's efforts.

Recommendations for Executive Action

Recognizing IRS's exploratory efforts are in their early stages and the Real Time Tax concept will likely evolve over time, we recommend the Acting Commissioner of Internal Revenue take the following actions to help ensure managers are able to assess the progress of exploratory efforts and have the information needed to weigh the potential risks, costs, and benefits of options:

- Identify time frames for the Real Time Tax exploratory effort's critical phases and essential activities.

- Develop a risk management framework for Real Time Tax that includes a record of risk analyses.

Agency Comments

We provided a draft of this report to the Acting Commissioner of Internal Revenue for comment. In written comments, reproduced in appendix V, IRS agreed with our recommendations. IRS said that as it continues to engage stakeholders and explore the Real Time Tax concept, it will identify time frames for critical phases and key activities and develop a risk management framework.

We are sending copies of this report to the Acting Commissioner of Internal Revenue. In addition, the report is available at no charge on the GAO website at http://www.gao.gov.

If you or your staff have any questions about this report, please contact me at James R. White at (202) 512-9110 or whitej@gao.gov. Contact points for our Offices of Congressional Relations and Public Affairs may be found on the last page of this report. GAO staff who made key contributions to this report are listed in appendix VI.

James R. White
Director, Tax Issues
Strategic Issues

Appendix I: Objectives, Scope, and Methodology

This appendix describes our methodology for addressing the following objectives: (1) describe when the Internal Revenue Service (IRS) receives and matches individual tax and information returns and (2) assess the extent to which IRS is following leading practices for managing an exploratory effort of this importance at IRS.

To describe when IRS receives and matches individual tax and information returns, we reviewed IRS documents and guidance, including the *Internal Revenue Manual* and IRS information return forms. We limited the scope of our review to the Form 1040 series[1] and the 25 information returns IRS officials said would likely be most relevant to matching to individual income tax returns under a Real Time Tax system.[2] We list these information returns in appendix II. Due to the manner in which IRS's Compliance Data Warehouse (CDW) consolidates data for Forms SSA-1099 and RRB-1099, we analyzed the combined data for these two returns. These two types of returns collectively accounted for 3.8 percent (59 million out of 1.6 billion returns) received by IRS for tax year 2011.

We generated descriptive statistics by accessing selected data elements from the CDW database, which provides a variety of tax return, enforcement, compliance, and other data. To develop information related to return volume, timing of return receipts and amendments, and refund issuance, we analyzed data for tax year 2011 returns, as this is the most

---

[1]The Form 1040 series includes, among others, Forms 1040 and 1040A, *U.S. Individual Income Tax Return*; 1040EZ, *Income Tax Return for Single And Joint Filers With No Dependents;* 1040-NR, *U.S. Nonresident Alien Income Tax Return*; 1040-PR, *Planilla para la Declaración de la Contribución Federal sobre el Trabajo por Cuenta Propia (Incluyendo el Crédito Tributario Adicional por Hijos para Residentes Bona Fide de Puerto Rico)*; and 1040-SS, *U.S. Self-Employment Tax Return (Including the Additional Child Tax Credit for Bona Fide Residents of Puerto Rico).* The 1040-PR is the Spanish version of the 1040-SS. In addition, Form 1040-SS is for use by bona fide residents of the U.S. Virgin Islands, Guam, American Samoa, and the Commonwealth of the Northern Mariana Islands.

[2]For the 25 information return types that we analyzed, 42 percent (415 million of 1 billion filed) of 1099-Bs and 51 percent (36 million of 70 million filed) of 1099-MISCs were issued to taxpayers identified by employer identification numbers rather than to individuals. We excluded these and other information returns that were issued to taxpayers with employer identification numbers, as IRS officials said these are not considered relevant to the Real Time Tax exploratory effort. For this same reason, we excluded other return types, such as Schedule K-1s. We also excluded other types of returns not used for matching against Form 1040s, such as Form FinCen 104, *Currency Transaction Report.*

recent year for which relatively complete data are available.[3] In analyzing
when tax returns were received by IRS, we used the cycle posting date,
when IRS posts tax return data to the master file, as it represents when
the tax return data are available for matching. Officials noted that IRS
must cleanse the data prior to posting to IRS systems. This may include
identifying and correcting incomplete or inaccurate data before posting
the data to IRS systems. To develop information related to the elapsed
time between matching information returns to income tax returns and
when IRS issued the first notice of discrepancy to taxpayers, we analyzed
data for tax year 2010 as this is the most recent year for which IRS has
completed the three phases of its matching process. We assessed the
reliability of CDW data by (1) performing electronic or manual testing of
required data elements to identify obvious errors, (2) reviewing existing
information about the data and the system that produced them, and (3)
interviewing agency officials knowledgeable about the data. We
determined that the data were sufficiently reliable for the purposes of this
report.

To assess the extent to which IRS is following leading practices for the
agency in its exploratory efforts, we reviewed IRS documents related to
the Real Time Tax exploratory effort, all of which were predecisional and
subject to change. Documents we reviewed included draft copies of the
Real Time Tax Conceptual Future Operating Model and the *Real Time
Tax Communications Strategy and Plan*. To further assess IRS's
approach, we identified leading practices that we consider relevant for
planning new initiatives at IRS using our past reports, *Standards for
Internal Control in the Federal Government*,[4] and IRS and other agency
documents, including the 2009 to 2013 *IRS Strategic Plan*. We then
compared IRS efforts to the leading practices we identified. The leading
practices we identified do not represent the universe of practices that IRS
could employ when planning a new initiative. We selected examples of
leading practices that we judged to be important for IRS to consider
during its Real Time Tax exploratory efforts. We discussed with IRS the
practices on which we based our descriptions and assessments during

---

[3]As returns may continue to be filed for tax year 2011 for 4 more years, the volume of
returns may continue to change somewhat in the future. Our analysis is based on return
data extracted from CDW April 17, 2013. IRS reviewed our information return counts as of
this date and confirmed that our data were substantially the same as their current counts.

[4]GAO, *Standards for Internal Control in the Federal Government*, GAO/AIMD-00-21.3.1
(Washington, D.C.: Nov. 1, 1999).

the course of our audit work, and IRS agreed with our approach. Officials
noted that they do not yet consider Real Time Tax a "project" and have
not decided whether to pursue Real Time Tax. A description of the
leading practices is detailed in appendix III.

We conducted this performance audit from August 2012 to June 2013 in
accordance with generally accepted government auditing standards.
Those standards require that we plan and perform the audit to obtain
sufficient, appropriate evidence to provide a reasonable basis for our
findings and conclusions based on our audit objectives. We believe that
the evidence obtained provides a reasonable basis for our findings and
conclusions based on our audit objectives.

Appendix II: Information Returns Used in Matching Against Individual Income Tax Returns

		Tax Year 2011 Due Dates		
			Due to IRS	
Form	Description	Due to Taxpayer	Paper	Electronic
1098	Filed by lenders to report mortgage interest of $600 or more. Certain points (prepaid interest on a mortgage loan) are also reported if the points, plus other interest on the mortgage, are $600 or more.	1/31/2012	2/28/2012	4/2/2012
1098-E	Filed by lenders to report student loan interest of $600 or more received.	1/31/2012	2/28/2012	4/2/2012
1098-T	Filed by eligible educational institutions and insurers (who make reimbursements or refunds) to report payments received or amounts billed for qualified tuition and related expenses.	1/31/2012	2/28/2012	4/2/2012
1099-A	Issued by lenders who acquire an interest in property that was security for a loan, or who know such property has been abandoned, to report income or loss.	1/31/2012	2/28/2012	4/2/2012
1099-B	Filed to report proceeds from broker and barter exchange transactions.	2/15/2012	2/28/2012	4/2/2012
1099-C	Filed by lenders to report cancelled debt of $600 or more.	1/31/2012	2/28/2012	4/2/2012
1099-DIV	Issued by banks and other financial institutions to report dividends and other distributions.	1/31/2012	2/28/2012	4/2/2012
1099-G	Filed by federal, state, and local government units to report payments of: unemployment compensation; state or local income tax refunds, credits or offsets; taxable grants; and/or agricultural payments.	1/31/2012	2/28/2012	4/2/2012
1099-INT	Filed to report interest income or U.S. Savings Bond and Treasury obligation interest of $10 or more, withholding for foreign taxes paid on interest, and backup withholding.	1/31/2012	2/28/2012	4/2/2012
1099-K	Issued by payment settlement entities to report merchant card payments and third-party network payments.	1/31/2012	2/28/2012	4/2/2012
1099-LTC	Filed by insurance companies, government units, and other providers to report long-term care benefits.	1/31/2012	2/28/2012	4/2/2012
1099-MISC[a]	Used to report miscellaneous income, such as: royalties or broker payments in lieu of dividends or tax-exempt interest of $10 or more; $600 or more in rents, services (including parts and materials), prizes and awards, medical and health care payments, crop insurance proceeds, cash payments for fish (or other aquatic life); fishing boat proceeds; gross proceeds paid to an attorney; direct sales of at least $5,000 of consumer products for resale from other than a permanent retail establishment; payments to independent contractors; directors' fees; commissions paid to lottery ticket sales agents; and backup withholding.	1/31/2012[b]	2/28/2012	4/2/2012

Form	Description	Tax Year 2011 Due Dates		
			Due to IRS	
		Due to Taxpayer	Paper	Electronic
1099-OID	Filed by financial institutions, brokers, and other entities to report the original issue discount (the excess of an obligation's stated redemption price at maturity over its issue price) includible in gross income of at least $10.	1/31/2012	2/28/2012	4/2/2012
1099-PATR	Filed by cooperatives to report payments of $10 or more in patronage dividends and other distributions, as well as any federal backup withholding.	1/31/2012	2/28/2012	4/2/2012
1099-Q	Filed by states or eligible educational institutions to report earnings or distributions from qualified tuition programs and Coverdell Education Savings Accounts.	1/31/2012	2/28/2012	4/2/2012
1099-R	Used to report distributions of $10 or more from pensions, annuities, individual retirement arrangements (IRAs), survivor income benefit plans, charitable gift annuities, and profit-sharing and retirement plans.	1/31/2012	2/28/2012	4/2/2012
1099-S	Used to report the sale or exchange of real estate.	2/15/2012	2/28/2012	4/2/2012
1099-SA	Used to report distributions from a health savings account, Archer Medical Savings Account, or Medicare Advantage Medical Savings Account.	1/31/2012	2/28/2012	4/2/2012
RRB-1099	Filed by the Railroad Retirement Board (RRB) to report Tier 1 railroad retirement benefits (the benefits railroad employees or beneficiaries would have been entitled to receive under the Social Security system) and special guaranty benefit payments.	1/31/2012	2/28/2012	4/2/2012
SSA-1099	Filed by the Social Security Administration (SSA) to report Social Security benefits.	1/31/2012	2/28/2012	4/2/2012
5498	Filed by the trustee or issuer of IRAs to report contributions, including any catch-up contributions, and the fair market value of the account.	5/31/2012[c]	5/31/2012	5/31/2012
5498-ESA	Used to report contributions, including rollover contributions, to any Coverdell Education Savings Account.	4/30/2012	5/31/2012	5/31/2012
5498-SA	Filed by a trustee or custodian of health savings accounts, Archer Medical Savings Accounts, and Medicare Advantage Medical Savings Accounts to report contributions, rollovers, and fair market value.	5/31/2012	5/31/2012	5/31/2012
W-2G	Filed to report certain gambling winnings and any federal income tax withheld on those winnings.	1/31/2012	2/28/2012	4/2/2012
W-2	Filed by employers to report wages paid to each employee from whom income, Social Security, or Medicare tax was withheld or from whom income tax would have been withheld if the employee had claimed no more than one withholding allowance or had not claimed exemption from withholding on Form W-4 (Employee's Withholding Allowance Certificate).	1/31/2012	[d]	[d]

Source: Analysis of IRS documents.

[a]The types of payments reportable on a 1099-MISC and their reporting thresholds vary widely. These include payments to nonemployees for services of at least $600 (called nonemployee compensation),

royalty payments of $10 or more, and medical and health care payments made to physicians or other suppliers (including payments by insurers) of $600 or more.

[b]If reporting substitute payments in lieu of dividends or interest or gross proceeds paid to an attorney, the due date was February 15, 2012.

[c]Provider must have furnished fair market value information and required minimum distribution, if applicable, to participants by January 31, 2012.

[d]Paper returns were due to the Social Security Administration by February 29, 2012, and electronic returns were due by April 2, 2012.

Appendix III: Leading Practices for Planning New Internal Revenue Service Initiatives

We have identified a number of leading practices for planning new initiatives at the Internal Revenue Service. Table 2 lists these leading practices and the sources used to develop them. As the table makes clear, we have applied these leading practices for a decade or more. In addition, our own review found these leading practices still relevant today. We discussed with IRS officials the leading practices on which we based our descriptions and assessments during the course of our audit work, and they agreed they are relevant to the Real Time Tax exploratory effort.

Table 2: Leading Practices for Planning New Internal Revenue Service Initiatives

Leading practices	Source
Dedicate a team to manage the process that • has the support of top leadership, • establishes support networks, and • is composed of a consistent and stable group of high-performing team members with the necessary knowledge and skills.	GAO. *Foreign Account Reporting Requirements: IRS Needs to Further Develop Risk, Compliance, and Cost Plans.* GAO-12-484. Washington, D.C.: April 16, 2012. GAO. *Patient Protection and Affordable Care Act: IRS Should Expand Its Strategic Approach to Implementation.* GAO-11-719. Washington, D.C.: June 29, 2011. GAO. *Information Technology: Critical Factors Underlying Successful Major Acquisitions.* GAO-12-7. Washington, D.C.: October 21, 2011. GAO. *Tax Administration: Planning for IRS's Enforcement Process Changes Included Many Key Steps but Can Be Improved.* GAO-04-287. Washington, D.C.: January 20, 2004. GAO. *Results-Oriented Cultures: Implementation Steps to Assist Mergers and Organizational Transformations.* GAO-03-669. Washington, D.C.: July 2, 2003.

Define program goals that
• link to the agency's mission,
• communicate a clear vision of the outcomes to be achieved,
• are established by key stakeholders who manage the program, and
• consider taxpayer burden by:
  ○ analyzing data on likely impacts on taxpayers before making decisions, and
  • working with stakeholders that will be important to implementing the initiative.
	GAO-11-719.
	
	GAO. *Government Reform: Goal Setting and Performance.* GAO/AIMD/GGD-95-130R. Washington, D.C.: March 27, 1995.
	
	U.S. Department of the Treasury. Internal Revenue Service. *IRS Strategic Plan 2009-2013.* http://www.irs.gov/pub/irs-pdf/p3744.pdf. Accessed August 20, 2012.
	
	GAO. *Internal Control Management and Evaluation Tool.* GAO-01-1008G. Washington, D.C.: August 1, 2001.

Leading practices	Source
Plan for performance measurement so that the agency can collect data needed for evaluating the program.	U.S. Department of the Treasury. Internal Revenue Service. *Internal Revenue Manual.* http://www.irs.gov/irm/. Accessed September 14, 2012.
	GAO-12-484.
	GAO-11-719.
	GAO-04-287.
	GAO. *Tax Administration: IRS Needs to Further Refine Its Tax Filing Season Performance Measures.* GAO-03-143. Washington, D.C.: November 22, 2002.
Establish a timeline that includes critical phases and essential activities for the planning effort.	GAO-12-484.
	GAO. *GAO Cost Estimating and Assessment Guide: Best Practices for Developing and Managing Capital Program Costs.* GAO-09-3SP. Washington, D.C.: March 2, 2009.
	GAO-03-669.

Establish a risk management framework.
• Comprehensively identify and analyze risks by
  • establishing a formal risk management procedure,
  • analyzing the consequences and likelihood of occurrence of identified risks, and assessing alternatives to mitigate risk.[a]
	GAO. *Patient Protection and Affordable Care Act: IRS Managing Implementation Risks, but Its Approach Could Be Refined.* GAO-12-690. Washington, D.C.: June 13, 2012.

	GAO-12-484.
	GAO-11-719.
	GAO-01-1008G.
	GAO. *Standards for Internal Control in the Federal Government.* GAO/AIMD-00-21.3.1. Washington, D.C.: November 1, 1999.
	GAO. *Risk Management: Further Refinements Needed to Assess Risks and Prioritize Protective Measures at Ports and Other Critical Infrastructure.* GAO-06-91. Washington, D.C.: December 15, 2005.
	Carnegie Mellon University, for the Software Engineering Institute. *Capability Maturity Model Integration for Acquisition, Version 1.3.* Hanscom Air Force Base, MA: November 2010.
Establish internal and external communications strategies. • Communicate both internally and externally program goals and operational changes before and as changes occur, • Solicit employee feedback and address concerns, and • Communicate a consistent message using a variety of media (e.g., e-mail, web, meetings).	U.S. Department of the Treasury. Internal Revenue Service. *IRS Strategic Plan 2009-2013.* http://www.irs.gov/pub/irs-pdf/p3744.pdf. Accessed August 20, 2012.
	GAO-12-484.
	GAO-12-7.
	GAO-11-719.
	GAO-01-1008G.
	GAO/AIMD-00-21.3.1

Source: GAO analysis.

Note: The leading practices we identified do not represent the universe of practices that IRS could employ when planning a new initiative. We selected examples of leading practices that we judged to be important for IRS to consider during its Real Time Tax exploratory efforts. We shared with IRS the practices on which we based our descriptions and assessments during the course of our audit work, and IRS agreed with our approach. Officials noted that they do not yet consider Real Time Tax a "project" and have not decided whether to pursue Real Time Tax.

[a]Cost-benefit analysis is critical in assessing alternatives, because it links the benefits derived from risk-reducing alternatives to the costs associated with implementing and maintaining them.

The figure below provides additional information on the amendment rates for the 25 information returns we reviewed.

Figure 8: Amendment Rate for Information Returns, Tax Year 2011

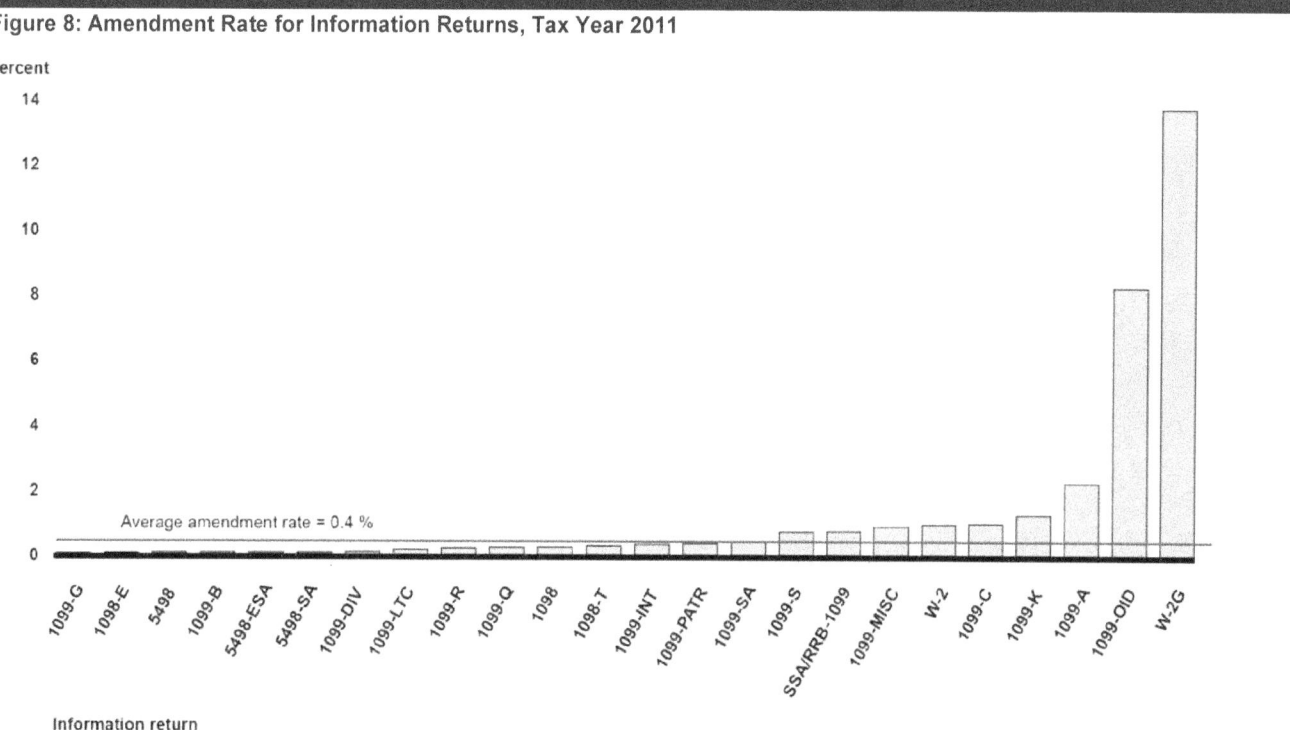

Information return

Source: GAO analysis of IRS data

Notes: Amendment rate is the percent of total volume attributed to amended, duplicate, and corrected returns. Since an individual return may be amended more than once, and an individual taxpayer may receive more than one type of information return that is amended, the volume of amendments received does not correspond to the number of unique taxpayers associated with the amendments.

Appendix V: Comments from the Internal Revenue Service

DEPARTMENT OF THE TREASURY
INTERNAL REVENUE SERVICE
WASHINGTON, D.C. 20224

DEPUTY COMMISSIONER

May 28, 2013

Mr. James R. White
Director, Strategic Issues
U.S. Government Accountability Office
441 G Street, N.W.
Washington, DC 20548

Dear Mr. White:

I have reviewed your draft report entitled *IRS Exploring Verification Improvements, But Needs To Better Manage Risks (GAO-13-515)*. I appreciate this comprehensive report that provides credible metrics and accurate reporting of activities to date on the IRS's real time tax exploratory effort. We agree with GAO's selection of leading practices for exploratory efforts, such as real time tax and appreciate acknowledgement of IRS' efforts in implementing four of the six leading practices selected.

The IRS also agrees with GAO's recommendation. As the IRS continues to engage stakeholders and explore the real time tax concept, we will identify timeframes for critical phases and key activities and develop a risk management framework.

If you have any questions, please contact me or members of your staff may contact Peter C. Wade, Associate Chief Information Officer for Enterprise Information Technology Project Management Office, at (404) 338-9086.

Sincerely,

Beth Tucker
Deputy Commissioner for
Operations Support

Enclosure

Enclosure

Recommendation:

Recognizing IRS's exploratory efforts are in their early stages and the Real Time Tax concept will likely evolve over time, we recommend the Acting Commissioner of Internal Revenue take the following actions to help ensure managers are able to assess the progress of exploratory efforts and have the information needed to weigh the potential risks, costs, and benefits of options.

- identify time frames for the Real Time Tax exploratory effort's critical phases and essential activities, and
- develop a risk management framework for Real Time Tax that includes a record of risk analyses.

Comment:

The IRS agrees with GAO that a timeline for critical phases and essential activities and a risk management framework, will help managers assess progress of the real time tax exploratory effort and provide the information needed to weigh potential risks, costs and benefits. We will address these items as the IRS continues to explore the real time tax concept.

Appendix VI: GAO Contact and Staff Acknowledgments

GAO Contact	James R. White, (202) 512-9110 or whitej@gao.gov.
Staff Acknowledgments	In addition to the contact named above, David Lewis (Assistant Director), Shannon Finnegan (Analyst-in-Charge), Ellen Rominger, Andrew Ching, and Albert Sim made key contributions to this report. Also contributing to this report were Joanna Berry, Jehan Chase, Michele Fejfar, Robert Gebhart, Robert Robinson, Sabrina Streagle, and John Zombro.